T0366875

WELFARE

JOHNS HOPKINS
UNIVERSITY PRESS

AARHUS UNIVERSITY PRESS

Welfare

CARSTEN JENSEN

WELFARE

© Carsten Jensen
and Johns Hopkins University Press 2023
Layout and cover: Camilla Jørgensen, Trefold
Cover photograph: Poul Ib Henriksen
Publishing editor: Karina Bell Ottosen
Translated from the Danish by Heidi Flegal
Printed by Narayana Press, Denmark
Printed in Denmark 2023

ISBN 978-1-4214-4474-1 (pbk)
ISBN 978-1-4214-4475-8 (ebook)

Library of Congress Control Number: 2022949353

Special discounts are available for bulk purchases of this
book. For more information, please contact Special Sales at
specialsales@jh.edu.

Published in the United States by:

Johns Hopkins University Press
2715 North Charles Street
Baltimore, MD 21218
www.press.jhu.edu

Published with the generous support of the
Aarhus University Research Foundation

Purchase in Denmark: ISBN 978-87-7219-188-1

Aarhus University Press
Helsingforsgade 25
8200 Aarhus N
Denmark
www.aarhusuniversitypress.dk

PEER
REVIEWED

MIX
Paper
FSC FSC® C010651

CONTENTS

'DENMARK, MY NATIVE LAND'

THERE'S NO PLACE LIKE HOME

The homeless man's gangrenous leg spread a sickly-sweet smell throughout the subway car. Newly embarked, I stood at the far end of the car with several other unwitting passengers, as far away from the poor, wretched man as I could get. At the next stop everyone hurried out, glad to leave the cloying stench behind. I never saw or heard of the man again. He must have died soon after.

When I tell other Danes about this incident in New York City, they typically exclaim: "My goodness, aren't we lucky to live in Denmark?" I have to reply: "Yes, we are." In Denmark the homeless man would not have faced a slow, undignified death noticed only, and with reluctance, by random passers-by. He would probably not even be homeless.

That episode took place in 2008. Seven years later I was once again in the United States for the presidential primaries. The remaining contenders for the Democratic nomination were Hillary Clinton and Bernie Sanders, and suddenly my native country was on everyone's lips.

When 'public welfare' came up in a televised debate,

Sanders said, "I think we should look to countries like Denmark, like Sweden and Norway, and learn what they have accomplished for their working people." "But we are not Denmark. I love Denmark," Clinton replied. "We are the United States of America."

As a Dane I was proud, but puzzled too: proud that two prominent American politicians gave the Danish welfare state positive mention; and puzzled that Clinton did not support Sanders in learning from Denmark and its Scandinavian siblings.

I soon learned myself that many Americans share Clinton's view, while Sanders is the odd man out. Advocates of welfare benefits for all are quickly labelled as 'socialists' touting a loony-left utopia. There is an ideological abyss here between Denmark and the US, which I have spent quite a bit of time studying.

On one side of the rift, my compatriots and I have become so thoroughly accustomed to living in a welfare state we can barely imagine life without it. Would Denmark even *be* Denmark, land that we love, without its all-embracing social security system? Curious foreigners often ask me about my country when they hear I am a Dane born and bred. In fact, my common surname, 'son of Jens', instantly reveals my ethnic roots. My personal list of other distinctly Danish things includes the cosy concept of *hygge*, a lovable film trio of small-time crooks called 'the Olsen Gang', a fairy-tale writer by the name of Hans Christian Andersen, communal singing and, yes, our welfare system – the feature that really makes Denmark stand out in the crowd.

You could say my story of the homeless man and the Sanders–Clinton exchange only confirm what Jens, Ole, Anders and lot of other Danes already knew: "Denmark, my native land" is simply the best place in the world. We all take good care of each other, and "few have too much; fewer still, not enough", as we sing in two well-known traditional songs.

Denmark *is* a good place to live. But tributes like these, from our 'Golden Age', soon take on a self-righteous, discordant tone when subjected to closer analysis. I use the word 'smugness' to describe this doubly sanctimonious faith in Denmark as (probably) the best *welfare state* in the world, and in our *motives* as the noblest ever.

After pondering Danish reactions to my subway story and Clinton's measured response to Sanders, I sincerely believe most Danes who hear them reflexively think: "How egoistic those Americans are!" Alas, the real world is far more complex.

A SUCCESS MADE IN DENMARK

Before I get too critical, I owe it to myself and my country to affirm that the Danish welfare state is a success story. It has more financial equality than most other countries in the world. These days, the wealthiest 1% of Americans are earning about three times as much as the wealthiest 1% of Danes. And not only are rich Americans richer than rich Danes; poor Americans are also poorer, and there are more of them, proportionately about twice as many as in Denmark.

Financial equality is not necessarily a goal in itself, but it does have various effects that most people see as positive. For instance, several studies show that parental income and education impact a child's future income and education more in the US than in Denmark. Small wonder, given that a good education in America (and many other countries) is pricey. One year's tuition at a decent university can easily cost 40,000 US dollars, living expenses not included. But the race begins much earlier, with wealthy parents often sending their children to expensive private schools rather than publicly funded alternatives.

Certainly, many talented Americans do better than their parents, but they are exceptions that confirm the rule – which, for most Americans, is that if they really want to live the American dream, they have to come to Denmark.

Inequality in health is also generally lower in Denmark than in the US, where most people have health insurance through their employer, with a higher pay cheque meaning better coverage.

The best insurance policies give almost unlimited access to private hospitals, therapy and expensive medication. Cheaper policies cover a smaller range of services, and if treatment costs exceed a certain limit, treatment is terminated, even if the patient has cancer, diabetes or other serious conditions.

Even Americans with prime coverage can end up struggling if they fall ill, especially if they lose their job – often their source of health insurance in the first place.

Unfortunate citizens with no health insurance have Medicaid, a public programme that covers certain at-risk groups, including underprivileged pregnant women. Even after the introduction of 'Obamacare' many millions are left without protection.

FOUR QUESTIONS AND A DEFINITION

For most of today's 5.9 million Danes, *equality* is the most defining trait in their special brand of 'welfare' – a term used in the positive sense of general happiness, health, well-being, prosperity and safety. Denmark has relatively few 'poor' people, and everyone has access to the same health care, education and old-age pension. But equality is not the only trait that sets Denmark and the rest of the Nordic region apart.

Welfare services in the Nordics are mainly provided by public institutions. In Denmark, for instance, the municipal authorities run the kindergartens and retirement homes, and the regional authorities run the hospitals. Hence the term 'welfare *state*'.

Many modern Danes use 'welfare services', 'welfare society', 'welfare state' and similar phrases interchangeably, without really considering the differences. Verbally and mentally merging such terms is another very Danish thing, and we do it almost instinctively. After all, the state, which fosters welfare and well-being, is our friend. Compare, again, with the US, where citizens are much more inclined to praise private initiative but reproach 'the government' for interfering in their lives.

The Danish welfare model is a success story because it has created a remarkable level of equality and forged strong links between the population and public institutions. This does not mean, however, that all is peachy in the state of Denmark.

In this book I reflect on four questions about the Danish welfare model. Each sheds light on certain aspects of it – some good, some debatable: Why do Danes support the welfare state? Which historic events and people have enabled such intimate links to arise between the state and our welfare? How much welfare do we actually get for our many tax *kroner*? And how has Denmark been able to combine welfare and wealth, and what of the system's viability in the future?

THE GOOD, THE BAD AND THE SANCTIMONIOUS

FISCAL CONSERVATIVES FOR WELFARE?

"We pay taxes to ensure that our welfare society can continue to run smoothly. But it is equally important for our welfare society to make sure that work pays off, and that we remain competitive in the future."

This quote, from the website of *Venstre* – the main fiscally conservative 'Liberal Party' of Denmark – explains the importance of lower tax on work incomes, the core party values being personal freedom and responsibility, and free competition. What many non-Danes will notice is not the implicit call for lower taxes, so that "work pays off" for the employee. That is fiscal conservatism 101. Rather, they will probably stumble over the implicit message that a person can have an equal or larger disposable income while *not* working but living on public benefits. Then, too, there is the premise, unexpected from a party nominally advocating fiscal prudence, that taxes "ensure … our welfare state."

As of 2023, all 12 parties in the Danish parliament, from left to right, support the idea of the welfare state. While they do this in different ways and disagree on key issues like taxation, the political consensus is that the welfare state is here to stay.

For instance, when Denmark's fiscal conservatives want to lower the top tax bracket, or national-patriotic politicians want to limit immigration from Muslim countries, they almost always refer to the necessity of such measures to ensure the survival of the welfare state – a common political cause, despite occasional calls for change.

And Danish voters agree. The Danish National Election Study, conducted since the early 1970s, has examined voter views on the welfare state. The scope and stability of support is remarkable. Consistently, a large majority of Danish respondents would like to maintain the welfare state in its current form. Many would even like spending on welfare services and benefits to grow.

The welfare state's popularity was perhaps expressed most clearly in 2016, with the publication of the *Denmark Canon – what makes us who we are*, a poll-based list of core cultural and social values. More than 325,000 Danes, quite a lot in our small population, voted online for one of 20 shortlisted values, including freedom, *hygge*, trust and welfare. The winner? Welfare – just ahead of freedom.

We Danes love our cradle-to-grave safety net. But why? If it were smaller, our tax rates – among the highest in the world, leaving many foreigners flabbergasted – could be much lower.

Besides high income taxes, Denmark also has sales taxes and duties on everything from food to cars to electricity, making living costs some of the highest anywhere. Economists compute a country's 'tax-to-GDP ratio' as taxes paid, all told, relative to the gross domestic product. According to the international think tank OECD, in 2021 Denmark took first place, slightly ahead of several Nordic neighbours, with an impressive 46.9%. In short, Danes handed over nearly half the value they produced that year to the tax authorities.

With lower taxes – like the 26.6% in the US, or the 29.9% in South Korea – we could decide how to spend our own hard-earned money instead of letting the state decide for us. Most Danes give little thought to the fact that we could easily organise our country quite differently. And frankly, who would not like to hand over *less* to the taxman?

There is no obvious reason why Danes should accept such high taxes, so how can we live with a system as onerous as the OECD numbers show? My research has revealed three possible explanations, which I call 'the good', 'the bad' and 'the sanctimonious'.

THE GOOD

Each year, hosts of Danes go through an online ritual, anxiously awaiting their turn on the website of *SKAT*, the Danish tax authority. Were their tax payments last year too large, too small or just right? Will they get a tax refund, or – heaven forbid – a residual tax notice? The latter can make even a Dane gripe and grumble. But almost magically, most of us routinely accept our assessment from *SKAT*. We may groan, but we do not question its validity, even if we have to cough up.

That is the first explanation: Danes accept high taxes because we trust our public institutions much more than most other nations do. By the way, although the taxman is no one's best friend, the word *skat* (pronounced like 'tax' backwards) also means 'treasure' – and 'dear' or 'beloved one'.

Indeed, our trust is not misplaced, as the Danish public sector is largely corruption-free. Citizens can count on receiving the public services they are entitled to, without helpful family ties or bribes.

In many other countries corruption is common. Even in wealthy European nations like France and Italy, personal contacts and networks can be decisive to the services a citizen receives.

Danes also see the allocation of welfare benefits and services as fair. That is because the Danish welfare state is *universal*, giving all citizens the same rights to hospital care, tuition-free education, an old-age pension and much more. If a new personal need arises – a citizen becomes ill, qualifies for university or must move to a residential care home – they automatically have a right to apply for the relevant public 'service intervention' or 'programme'.

Not so outside Scandinavia, where often there is no direct link between citizens' needs and the public services they receive, as in the case of the homeless man with the putrid leg.

The Danish welfare state is popular because we

trust our well-run public systems, essentially with good reason. However, in recent years a spate of public-sector problems have come to light: faulty IT and property assessment systems, tax fraud, misappropriation, extravagant spending and plain old laxity. This could undermine our trust in the state, though by international standards Danes still place great trust in their public institutions.

What makes Denmark special is the way the national, regional and local governments work together, and the 'good' explanation for the welfare state's popularity is that an equitable, orderly public sector merits the population's support. The next explanation is very different and much less flattering.

THE BAD

A recurring scene plays out in early August every year at every community school in Denmark: 'first school day' for new pupils. Muted anticipation. Fidgeting. Colourful classrooms with tiny chairs, and sipping of red fruit juice from plastic cups during the new teacher's words of welcome. On-the-spot news reporting, as though this were anything new. I remember my own first day at school. How proud I was to already know 'a' and 'b', *and* 'c', which boded well for my future.

This ritual, a big day for pupils and parents, is also symbolic of the welfare state's role in Danish daily life, providing services from cradle to grave. Expecting mothers (and fathers) get prenatal care and classes, and the hospital takes care of the birth. Newborns are regularly checked at home by a public health visitor, also free of charge. After a year or so of paid or subsidised maternity (or paternity) leave, parents are guaranteed a spot for their child in a day-care facility (co-financed by parents), before the child moves on to school, and often to tuition-free vocational training or academic study. Old, infirm family members receive care services at home or in one of the country's many residential care homes.

Much of the Danish welfare system serves the middle class, helping them to live 'the good life'. The few who do *not* dip into the welfare cornucopia are seen by the many as either too rich or too idealistic – raising eyebrows in either case.

The 'bad' explanation for the welfare state's popularity is simple. There's something in it for us Danes. We love the welfare state because it helps us live comfortable middle-class lives without too much of an effort.

This analysis may sound like gratuitous criticism coming from a researcher working at a publicly funded Danish university, but our findings suggest it is sound. As I mentioned, most Danes wish to see even more spent on welfare, but this wish is conditional, as standard cradle-to-grave services enjoy far more support than services that do *not* benefit the middle class.

A good example is the 'cash benefit', the means-tested social assistance paid to the neediest citizens. Only about 20% of Danes wish to see more spent on cash-benefit redistribution, while just as many wish the opposite.

Meanwhile, when asked about hospital care, 60–70% of respondents want more spending. The rest prefer the current level, while virtually none want less.

Several researchers have exposed an unbecoming trend: Danes primarily support welfare measures they believe will benefit *them*. Take seniors, who look more favourably on the universal old-age pension than younger citizens. This unsurprising finding nonetheless underscores that the welfare model does not rest on noble motives alone. Self-insight is always healthy, but it does little to bolster our self-image. Fortunately, we have now arrived at my third and last explanation: the sanctimonious one.

THE SANCTIMONIOUS

This last explanation, rooted in smugness, revolves around the Danes as a people.

'A people' is a group who share an ethnic origin, language, culture and history. Danes fulfil these criteria, as they have since Denmark emerged from the mists of history over a thousand years ago. The question is: Does this have a bearing on our thinking about welfare? Is there something unique about us *as Danes*? Some believe there is.

Two of the many who eulogised Danishness in the 1800s were the poet Adam Oehlenschläger (1779–1850) and the theologian, writer and educator NFS Grundtvig (1783–1872). Obviously, neither wrote of the welfare state, which arose long after they had turned to dust, but both figures helped shape and inspire the way Danes think about who we are, as Danes, and how greatly we value equality and mutual trust.

Grundtvig – who founded the Danish folk high school movement and wrote the lyrics of many of its 'life-enlightening' songs, which are still sung today – put it succinctly in this passage from his classic ode 'Far higher are mountains elsewhere on the earth' from 1820:

> But Danes never lack for their own daily bread,
> no less in the poor peasant's dwelling.
> In this lies our wealth, on this tenet we draw:
> that few are too rich, and still fewer too poor.

This brand of national-romantic poetry claims that at some point Danes developed a special culture of equality, perhaps after the agrarian reform movement and Grundtvig's 'life enlightenment' work in the 1800s, or the sweeping cooperative movement around 1900, or perhaps even in the Viking Age around the year 1000. Whatever the case, the Grundtvig quote above evidences some sort of long-standing equality culture.

These theoretical explanations do not suffice, however. Today we know that Danish equality is a new phenomenon. A century ago the richest Danes earned about four times what they do today, compared to the rest of the population. In fact, there was little or no difference between the richest people in America and Denmark – although the latter were a tad richer than their peers in the US. In other words, if Denmark did have some sort of 'equality culture' it had no bearing on financial equality and was worth little in that respect.

One variety of this notion of a 'special Danish equality culture' emphasises the way Danes typically trust others, beyond their family and friends. Political scientists call this kind of trust 'social trust', and some of my colleagues actually think social trust may be a Danish trait that is several centuries old.

But wait a minute: Although a recent study showed that Danes were among the most trusting people in the world, that too is a new phenomenon. In 1979, for the first time ever, researchers gathered scientific data on social trust in Denmark. The score was much lower than today, with less than half of respondents stating they generally trusted other people. The corresponding figure these days is around 80%.

What is more, in 1979 the Danish social-trust score was as low as the American score that year, so if high social trust is part of Denmark's millennium-long cultural history, it seems odd that it was so low just 40 years ago. I find it equally odd that social-trust levels can apparently fluctuate wildly over mere decades. Looking to other fields, archaeologists and historians rarely, if ever, associate such dramatic shifts with ancient cultural patterns.

HOW TO FLEECE A TAX LAMB

How can Danes endure being fleeced by the taxman

year after year? Of the three explanations I proposed, the last – the smug and sanctimonious one – does not suffice, whereas the two others play a role. We happily, or at least willingly, pay our taxes because the welfare state is an integral part of our daily lives and helps where help is needed, and also because public institutions and employees go by the book.

This explains the continuing popularity of the welfare state, despite the high tax burden. But how did the welfare state arise? A good question, particularly if I am right in saying there is nothing special about the Danish people. If there is not something special about us, then why did Denmark end up with such a special welfare state?

COMPROMISES, CHURCH REGISTERS AND KITCHEN SINKS

FROM CLASS STRUGGLE TO CONSENSUS

The Copenhagen bricklayers had long been on strike to reduce their workday from 11 hours to 10. Their strike fund was almost gone. The legendary Danish labour-movement leader Louis Pio called a fundraising rally on the Common, the city's largest park. The police, fearing unrest, prohibited the rally, but to no avail.

On 5 May 1872 the thousands who assembled on the Common were attacked by police and troops. It was a bloody day for Denmark. The number of injured workers is unknown, but the authorities recorded 97 wounded police officers and soldiers in what became known as the Battle on the Common.

This clash heralded a new age of workers refusing to be exploited with long hours and miserable wages. Slowly but surely the social unrest of the 1870s gave rise to the Danish *labour movement*.

Today, 150 years later, the labour movement is still fighting for workers' rights and organising workers in trade unions, of which Denmark has several. Representing their members in official talks with corporate employers, unions enable workers to stand together, go on strike and negotiate better conditions.

Earlier, a grumbling worker could simply be sacked and replaced. But workers 'in union' can strike: No one comes to work, so the employer's factory stands idle, making no money. This can bring even the most stubborn capitalist to the bargaining table.

A year before the Battle on the Common, the Social Democratic Party was founded, with Pio as a driving force. Like the unions, the party fought to improve workers' conditions but did so through legislative efforts, not industrial action. For decades the party had little political influence, but in 1924 the Social Democrats formed their first government, led by a prime minister named Thorvald Stauning, also legendary in later years. His government lasted just two years, but 1929 was the dawn of Danish social democracy's glory days – 50 years of them.

Other countries, including Norway and Sweden, also had large unions and strong social democratic parties. Social scientists have shown that the stronger a country's labour movement, the wider the scope of its public welfare services. It is hardly coincidental that Norway and Sweden also evolved into welfare states, and that researchers speak of the 'Scandinavian welfare model'.

But Danes grateful for today's welfare services must look beyond the labour movement. It was certainly strong in Denmark, but it did not have absolute power. The unions could never compel employers to bow down, and the Social Democratic Party never won an absolute parliamentary majority in the 179-seat *Folketing*.

It did come close though, winning 46.1% of the total vote in the 1935 general election. Although impressive, this is not good enough if you want to call all the shots. As a result, the labour movement had to hammer out one compromise after another with its political opponents, not least the two fiscal and value-oriented conservative parties.

The first noteworthy accord was the September Compromise of 1899, which came about after the biggest labour conflict in Danish history. Over half of the country's organised workers were locked out for 100 days, employers refusing to let workers in until they accepted what was on offer. Neither side would budge.

Ultimately, the employers recognised the unions as the workers' legal representatives, and the unions accepted the employers' right to 'manage and allocate tasks in the workplace'. The September Compromise came to define the Danish labour market's modus vivendi for much of the 1900s and, to some extent, does so to this day. The two sides would negotiate or 'collectively bargain' directly, with no interference from politicians or government officials.

The next pivotal compromise came three decades later, with the Kanslergade Accord of 1933. Denmark's economy was in a slump. Agriculture – then the country's most important sector – saw a drop in exports of bacon and other products to the UK. The whole country was hurting as unemployment and poverty soared.

The crisis in Germany was just as grave, and the National Socialist Party, led by Adolf Hitler, was skipping from one electoral victory to the next, as contending parties appeared paralysed and incompetent. If the democratic parties in Germany's small northern neighbour had proved incapable of handling the crisis, the same might have happened there. In short, Denmark's future as a democracy hung in the balance.

Thorvald Stauning was once again prime minister of a coalition government. After gruelling negotiations in Stauning's own home in Kanslergade street, he engineered a compromise with the fiscally conservative Liberal Party, which traditionally represented farmers and was not 'liberal' in the modern sense of the word. The gist of the Kanslergade Accord was that Stauning agreed to devalue the Danish *krone*, making the country's agricultural products relatively cheaper in the UK and boosting sales from Denmark. In return, the Social Democrats were given various concessions that greatly boosted social rights. As Stauning later exclaimed: "We have sacrificed some principles, but we have saved the country!" The manoeuvre worked and the party won a landslide victory in the 1935 general election under the slogan "Stauning – or *Chaos.*"

Twenty-three years later, in 1956, Danish politicians reached the country's third great compromise. The issue at stake was a universal 'people's pension', the *folkepension*, an idea promoted after World War II by the country's Social Liberal Party, which found the existing old-age pension inadequate. The Social Democrats, although in favour, held that any improvements must only benefit the poorest citizens – the working class, meaning their own voters.

Understandably, the Liberal Party and Conservative Party refused to vote for a pension reform that would not benefit *their* voters, and such a reform would be unviable in the long term if a Liberal–Conservative coalition changed or scrapped it when they came to power. The result: a 'universal old-age pension' paying a guaranteed minimum to all Danes over 67 – regardless of income and personal wealth – with extras for the poorest citizens.

The September Compromise, the Kanslergade Accord and the universal old-age pension accord are cornerstones in the Danish welfare system. All three show a Danish labour movement strong enough to set the bargaining agenda, but not strong enough to dictate the outcomes. The result is a very particular type of consensus in which even centre-right parties stand behind the welfare state.

THE SUPERORDINARY COMMISSION OF OVE RODE

Let me share some important digits with you: 0, 8, 1, 0, 8 and 0. Besides these, my date of birth, there are four other digits I shall keep to myself. Otherwise I would unwisely reveal my whole 'CPR number' – the unique personal identifier in our Danish welfare system. Everybody in Denmark has one. A CPR number is the key that links one specific person to public databases that hold a wealth of information: addresses, public health-care records, tax statements ... Think of it as exhaustive, up-to-date census information and much more, available at any time – but in tiny bits, and only to the select few authorised to access it. These include Statistics Denmark, public administrators, health-care employees and researchers like myself.

The CPR number was introduced in 1968 as a tool to improve the welfare state. Well, actually it was a tool to rake in even more tax *kroner* to pay for welfare services. The technical key to all this was 'source tax'.

Before 1968, working Danes received their full pay from their employer. Company bookkeepers deducted no taxes for transfer to the authorities, so at year-end each employee personally had to calculate how much they owed in taxes, then spend the following year paying off their tax debt. The system was hopeless.

For one thing, to complete a tax-return form – on paper – each citizen had to keep full details of their incomes and tax deductions, then do some highly complex calculating. For another, short-changing the proverbial taxman was fairly easy, since verifying a specific citizen's earnings was hard.

Source tax, introduced by a conservative finance minister in 1970, solved the problem. Henceforth, a company's bookkeepers would deduct the employees' income tax, pay the taxman, then pay the rest to the employee – but this was only possible if *SKAT* knew all about Mr. Hansen's place of work and pay packet. Otherwise, how would *SKAT* know whether Mr. Hansen had paid his taxes? That is why, to this very day, the CPR number is the unit that links all company pay offices in Denmark to the IT systems at *SKAT*.

A CPR number. Source tax. How dull these words sound! But make no mistake. In countless ways they epitomise the Danish public administration's ability to solve complex problems, and to do this so efficiently that Danes barely think about what it really takes to run the system we have.

In historical terms, the CPR number is the apex of a long evolutionary process. In 1646, the notable king Christian IV (1577–1648) ordered all pastors in the realm's official Lutheran state church to keep a 'parish ledger' and record all christenings, confirmations, engagements, marriages and deaths in the parish. With the 'public sector' being undeveloped to non-existent, the pastor was the only 'public employee' most communities had.

This changed little until the early 1900s, with World War I as a painful turning point. Due to near-universal shortages, the government had to severely ration everything from coffee beans to machine components, calling for strict control. The political effort was led by the social-liberal minister of domestic affairs, Ove Rode, who set up a 'Superordinary Commission' to handle the task. Although rationing was not popular, the Danes became used to 'the state' intervening to solve large societal problems.

Many other countries went through similar processes, but several unusual circumstances were at work in Denmark. First and foremost, the parties in power represented movements broadly rooted in *folket* – the people.

As noted, the labour movement's political arm was the Social Democratic Party. The other sweeping movement was the *farmers' movement*, politically linked to the Liberal Party and the Social Liberal Party. In fact, since 1901 all Danish prime ministers – with a single brief but notable exception in 1920 – have belonged to one of these three parties.

But back to the labour and farmers' movements, which were backed and run by ordinary Danes. Their activities went far beyond politics to include sports associations, cooperative retailing, the building and running of folk high schools and much more. That is why, politically, it was natural for the social-democratic, fiscally conservative and social-liberal parties to promote people's involvement in self-organised activities. They wanted citizens to have certain things the state did *not* handle for them.

Even today Denmark has one of the world's highest rates of club and association membership. Furthermore, a third of the population regularly volunteer, often at local sports clubs or to help people in need, such as disadvantaged children, homeless people and elderly citizens. It is interesting that a nation so blanketed in welfare services has so many active volunteers too.

There are other areas where the state plays a lesser role in providing welfare. One is the collective unemployment funds that pay benefits to members. These are run by the unions – which, until 2009, also had to help jobless members find work – so labour organisations handle several tasks related to welfare in Denmark.

KITCHEN SINK, OR SWIM?

The time has come to create the framework for a labour market that leaves more room to consider families. Today, far too many families with young children live a hectic life, in some cases too hectic. We have all seen young parents – most often it's the mother – arriving on their bicycles at the day-care facility in the dark of early morning, their toddlers half-asleep in the child seats behind them.

These lines are from a Danish prime minister's national New Year's address. Even most Danes would be hard pressed to say who uttered them, and when. Anker Jørgensen, a constant, classic Social Democrat, in the 1970s? Or Lars Løkke Rasmussen, the recent Liberal Party PM? Or Mette Frederiksen, head of a modern Social Democratic minority government since the general election in 2019? The reason is that this quote encapsulates several key principles of the Danish welfare system.

First, Danish women work – hence the early-morning bicycle ride. Second, Denmark has public crèches and kindergartens to care for kids while parents work – hence the toddlers in the child seats.

In today's Denmark, more than 90% of children aged 1–3 attend some sort of day care, the vast majority for 30 hours or more per week. This is a world record. Even Norwegian and Swedish parents spend more time with their children than Danish parents do.

Many children across Europe are cared for at home, by their mothers, until they start school. While this may benefit the child, it means the woman must stop working after childbirth. If siblings follow, the career hiatus can last a decade or more.

In addition, many new mothers are just getting started at work, so they will go back later with little or no experience and a potentially obsolete education – if they got their degree at all. This sort of predicament often keeps women at home, or gets them poorly paid part-time jobs. Put bluntly, child-minding services are vital to gender equality in employment. So how did Denmark end up with publicly run, state-subsidised childcare? Quite simply, perfect timing.

From 1958 to 1973, Denmark saw the largest sustained economic upswing ever, averaging 5% economic growth each year. With unemployment at a record low, Danish companies faced a serious shortage of labour.

Jens Otto Krag, the country's Social Democratic prime minister for much of the 1960s, soon realised where the solution lay: at the kitchen sink. If even a fraction of homemakers took a job, Denmark's workforce would be adequate to keep the country afloat. Krag appointed a commission to determine how to help women join the workforce. It soon concluded that childcare was the answer to virtually all of Krag's prayers. From the mid-1960s the number of day-care facilities – 'day institutions' – began to rise, and it gradually became easier to strike a good work–life balance.

But it takes two to tango, and the call for women to work coincided with a cultural revolution that washed across Denmark and much of the Western world, challenging traditional gender roles. Women increasingly wanted good educations and prominent positions, too. In 1955 only around 10% of university graduates were women. Twenty years later this number had almost tripled, and about 50% more women aged 15–69 worked outside the home.

Krag and other politicians, mainly from the left, boosted this trend, as droves of Danish women gladly left the kitchen sink to swim in the tidal wave of women's liberation. Young families demanded even better day-care options for small children. Crèches, kindergartens, months of paid maternity and parental leave, paid absence on the first day of a child's sick spell … These all became and remain part of Denmark's core welfare services.

In Germany, Italy and elsewhere it was still unacceptable in the 1960s and 1970s for women to *want* to leave the kitchen sink. The church was strong, and many Christian-democratic governments fought to maintain traditional values like work-away fathers and stay-at-home mothers. Tradition now means less, but for many in southern Europe, 'homemaker' remains the ideal female role. The result is limited day-care options, and thus less gender equality.

Now back to where this section began: a microquiz about a quote. It is from a speech given in 1998 by Social Democratic prime minister Poul Nyrup Rasmussen – incidentally one of three Danish PMs since 1993 to bear that surname. In total, between 1993 and 2019 these three unrelated 'sons of Rasmus' governed Denmark for 22 years.

RIGHT TIME, RIGHT PLACE, RIGHT EVERYTHING

You have probably heard the tale of *Goldilocks and the Three Bears*, about a little girl who visits the home of Papa Bear, Mama Bear and Baby Bear, who have gone out for a walk. Goldilocks, clearly a girl of very particular habits, tries out their chairs and even tastes the porridge on the table, which awaits the bear family's return. Baby Bear's porridge has cooled to perfection, so she gobbles it up. Tired from her exploits, she tries out the three beds upstairs. Again, Baby Bear's is not too hard, not too soft, but just right, and Goldilocks falls into a deep sleep.

Folk tales always have a strong message, but the moral of the story is not my point here. My point is how everything falls into place as Goldilocks moves through her perfect afternoon – until the angry bears chase her away, of course. So, too, certain things in Danish history fell into place, and the welfare state grew out of very particular conditions with just the right amount of three factors: a strong labour movement, but not too strong; a strong state, but not too strong; and perfect timing as an epic Danish upswing coincided with women's liberation. None of these three conditions alone can explain Denmark's current welfare system. All three must come into play and be in balance, just like the three factors leading up to that perfect nap.

The Danish welfare state is, in many ways, one of a kind. The reason, however, is not that Danes as a people are unique, or that some uniquely brilliant politician decided to construct the welfare-state model we now have. As I explained, it is more a case of random but auspicious historical circumstances.

But enough of the past. Let us move on to the future, for no matter how we ended up here, the results of the Danish welfare state are fabulous: equality, happiness and harmony. Or are things really that simple?

LONG LIVE THE CLASS SOCIETY!

A TOUR OF AARHUS AND ENVIRONS

I have lived in Aarhus for quite a few years now. It is a lovely little city, Denmark's second largest and home to some 330,000 souls. I love to walk through the many distinctive neighbourhoods and beyond. A brisk two-hour jaunt can get me from my home in the heart of Aarhus to just about anywhere I want to go – the suburbs new and old, the forests to the north and south, the broad bay to the east or the large lake to the west – and back again.

As I roam and ramble, I also tour the Danish class society, for make no mistake: Denmark is by no means classless. Taking a look at where and how people live speaks volumes about their financial situations and their lives in general.

This may sound like a paradox. I just told you about the universal public welfare system that serves all Danes, yet within walking distance of my home, I can find remarkable inequality. Just a few kilometres from Risskov, an affluent suburb near the forest north of the city, lies Gellerup, where unemployment is high. Everyone living in Risskov and Gellerup has access to the same welfare services – so why does inequality still exist in Denmark?

MONEY MAKES THE WORLD GO AROUND

Although geographically close, Gellerup and Risskov are
a world apart. There are similar neighbourhoods across
the globe, and your town or city is probably no exception.

The Gellerup Project is a social housing area
consisting mainly of large blocks of concrete flats
from the late 1960s and early 1970s. Over the years the
Municipality of Aarhus and the housing associations have
tried to renovate façades and outdoor spaces in Gellerup,
but although recent urban-renewal projects are breaking
the uniformity, a certain lacklustre air prevails.

Much of Risskov is old villas and large homes near
the beach and the forest. Most are handsome and well
maintained, with lovely gardens and an Audi or two in the
garage. It is one of Denmark's most prestigious suburbs,
and real estate prices are sky high.

Calculations from the Economic Council of the
Labour Movement, a Danish thinktank, show that
average household earnings, per annum, are 3.3 times
higher in Risskov than in Gellerup. After tax. Although
Copenhagen, Odense and Aalborg show similar patterns,
this is the largest gap in Denmark. Not surprisingly,
smaller cities and towns show smaller differences, simply
because their inhabitants are more homogeneous.

Large gaps occur not only *within* cities, towns
and municipalities but also *among* municipalities in
different parts of the country. Households in the richest
municipalities have an average income, after tax, that is

roughly twice as high as that of households in the poorest municipalities.

The geographical pattern is clear. The richest municipalities are in North Zealand and East Jutland – north of Copenhagen, and around Aarhus – while the poorest are in outlying areas. This belt of Danish 'fringe areas' roughly curves around North, West and South Jutland, then runs across the lower part of Funen and the southern islands, over to Bornholm in the Baltic. Due to its shape, this swathe of peripheral areas has rather unkindly been dubbed 'the Rotten Banana'.

Obviously, not all households in affluent municipalities earn more than the national average. Still, the trend is clear. People with good jobs and high incomes – doctors, lawyers, engineers – tend to gather in a few places, even more so today than two or three decades ago. Since 1985 the average household income, after tax, has swelled all of 127.8% in Gentofte, compared to a rise of just 36.8% in Brøndby, a bit southwest of Copenhagen. All Danes have become richer, but some more than others.

In the total population, again after tax, the poorest tenth earns 3.6% of all incomes, whereas the richest tenth earns 22.5%. Here, too, there is a rising trend compared to 1985, when the poorest tenth earned 4.2% of all incomes, but the richest tenth only 17.9%.

This lopsided picture becomes even clearer if we look at the personal assets of the Danes – the value of their homes, deposit accounts, pensions and shares. Statistics show that the richest tenth own 48% of all private assets in Denmark. When we leave all pension assets out of the equation, the imbalance only grows, putting nearly two thirds of assets in the hands of the richest tenth of the population.

"TOTALLY RIDICULOUS"

If you find yourself at a Danish dinner party with an irrepressible urge to ruin the conversation, do not bring up sex or religion, which are usually not problematic topics for Danes. Instead, bring up poverty. For maximum impact, base your statement on the host's political views.

To rile a fiscally conservative or right-leaning host, try putting on a concerned foreign-observer expression and say: "I must admit, I'm quite surprised to see so many poor people around. I thought Denmark was a welfare state?" Inversely, if your host is left-leaning, feign mild outrage and exclaim: "By the way, just yesterday at a café I overheard some Danes complaining about 'poverty' among unemployed professionals – who get more in benefits every month than I make working full time. 'Poor people' in Denmark? You've got to be kidding!"

A well-chosen remark on this topic can tick off even the suavest of Danes, since we cannot seem to agree on what poverty is. There are, in fact, two varieties: *absolute poverty* and *relative poverty*. The former means a person is so poor they cannot afford basic necessities: food, potable water, clothing and shelter. The latter means a person does not have enough money to maintain a dignified lifestyle on a par with the rest of the population.

Clearly, absolute poverty is minimal in Denmark. To my knowledge, people do not die of starvation in my country, and practically everyone has a roof over their head. In 2019, the Danish Center for Social Science Research numbered the country's homeless at 6,400, or about 0.1% of the population. Not considering the personal tragedy of homelessness, which is often exacerbated by mental illness and substance abuse, for Danish society as a whole, homelessness is a minor problem.

Defining relative poverty is much more difficult. How does one measure something as intangible as 'a dignified lifestyle'? In 2013 Karen Hækkerup of the Social Democrats, then minister of social affairs and integration, issued an 'official poverty line' for Denmark: an annual 103,200 *kroner* (13,800 euros) for a one-person household, or 8,600 *kroner* (1,170 euros) per month, after tax. The poverty line was later abolished, but let us spend a few moments on it anyway.

Denmark is generally expensive to live in, and to visit, and most Danes would find it hard to pay rent and other costs of living – food, utilities and insurance – on a disposable monthly income of just 8,600 *kroner*. I kid you not. Life's little luxuries would be history: no daily newspaper, no visits to a café or restaurant and definitely no ski holiday in February.

So how many CPR-card-carrying residents of

Denmark lived below the 2013 poverty line? The criteria were: at least three years with a post-tax annual income below 103,200 *kroner*, and total personal assets of less than 100,000 *kroner*. Note that students – who pay no tuition and get a monthly student allowance called SU from the state – were excluded. Economists estimated in the early 2010s that, out of 5.9 million, about 40,000 Danes lived in poverty. This sounds like a lot, considering Denmark's reputation as the world champion in welfare services.

When Minister Hækkerup's 'official poverty line' bill was passed, it caused a ruckus. One critic, Joachim B. Olsen of the fiscal hard-liner party Liberal Alliance, labelled it "totally ridiculous". When the Liberal Party regained power in 2015, the poverty line was predictably abolished. More recently, Denmark has been obliged by the UN to introduce a poverty line for statistical reasons – but one that has not yet been authorized by the government as 'official'.

Many disliked the official poverty line, feeling it signalled that all Danes must have access to precisely the same opportunities, 'in equal measure' right down to the tiniest crumb. But is someone poor because they cannot afford to join a sports club, own a car or go on holiday abroad?

None of us can answer objectively, for we all have political convictions. And that is precisely why 'poverty' is the perfect topic to ruin any Danish dinner party, should you feel the urge.

ONWARDS AND UPWARDS!

It is no use denying that some Danes have more money than others; some a lot more. But does this influence the way people are able to live their lives? Obviously, some own a posh villa and drive a new BMW; others rent a flat and drive an old jalopy. But the crucial question is whether parental background influences a child's future. The short answer is, 'Yes, absolutely.'

In a Danish context this is not self-evident, with a welfare system designed to give everyone equal opportunities to get an education and find a job that suits their abilities. Even so, Denmark's welfare state is startlingly unsuccessful at breaking chains of negative social inheritance.

Researchers studied a group of Danes, aged 15–16 in the mid-1990s, whose parents, at that time, were jobless most of the year. Ten years later, 37% of this group had no education at upper-secondary level or above. Young people whose parents work are far more likely to complete an education, but class impacts this statistic, too. Children of medical consultants more often complete an education than children of health-care assistants, and the degrees they earn most often lead to large salaries and long careers.

If, say, a health-care assistant's daughter completes training and becomes a shop assistant, she can look forward to total lifetime earnings of 13 million *kroner* (around 1.7 million euros), after tax, if she works up to retirement in her late sixties.

If, instead, she becomes a 'social educator', of which Denmark has many, she will earn virtually the same: 13.2 million. If you think this sounds like a whole sack full of cash, then tell the medical consultant's son to bring a wagon. If he gets, say, a degree in civil engineering, he could rake in 24.5 million or so. But if his social inheritance, in the positive sense, is a career in medicine, he can look forward to a comfortable 31 million *kroner* in his lifetime, after tax – plus his universal old-age pension, obviously.

Money cannot and should not be used as a universal measuring stick, but such disparities are noteworthy. What is more, Danes with long educations continue to work longer. Regardless of gender, the average social educator will work for 32.5 years; the average doctor for 38.7 years.

Another category, non-skilled workers, are only active on the labour market for an average of 22.3 years, for two reasons. First, many non-skilled people never gain a solid footing in their workplaces. Second, non-skilled workers with a permanent job are more often approved for early retirement than other Danes.

Many young people do better than one might expect from their social background, and many people do very well in life without an academic degree. Denmark *is* a land of equal opportunity compared with much of the world. Still, the fact remains that the most crucial *non*-choice in the lives of most people, including Danes, is who our mothers and fathers are.

ADDING INSULT TO EQUALITY

When I use the terms 'equal' and 'opportunity' about Denmark, what I mean is: Denmark is more equal than most other countries, making us 'relatively equal'. So, despite differences, our sweeping welfare system and social safety net catch the jobless and disadvantaged before they hit rock bottom. But the welfare state does *not* create total equality – not by any measure.

So is this inequality a problem? The question is largely a moral one. Many left-leaning politicians find it wrong to offer people such dissimilar life conditions, just because they were born into a certain family. Most right-leaning politicians believe people should take their own destiny in hand and not use their family background as an excuse to shirk and sulk. Ill-starred upbringing or not, it is *your* life.

Both views are based on moral principles, and both are found in the political landscape. That is why there is no ultimate 'right answer' to either spending more on welfare to further reduce inequality or, alternatively, limiting welfare services and increasing inequality. At any rate, my peers and I cannot find an ultimate answer through research. Instead, politicians must make decisions based on what the majority of Danes find right or wrong – as voiced every four years or so in a general election.

That is why sensational news stories in Denmark are not based on general reports of growing inequality and poorer living conditions for many Danes, which, although factually observable, are seen as abstract technicalities. Illustrating the contrary, two major media sensations this past decade have revolved around specific Danes now known, respectively, as 'Poor Carina' and 'Lazy Robert'.

Poor Carina shot to fame in 2011, in Denmark and abroad, after explaining her financial situation in a popular television talk show. A recipient under the social-assistance programme known as 'cash benefits' and a single mother, Carina had just under 16,000 *kroner* (2,150 euros) a month at her disposal, after tax. After overheads, including food, Carina had about 5,000 *kroner* a month to spend on herself and her son. Many fiscally conservative voices found this amount insultingly high, with Denmark's low wage earners in mind.

In the other camp, Carina herself and various left-wing politicians held that she was, in fact, 'poor', perhaps not in absolute terms, but due to her inability to maintain a 'dignified lifestyle' for herself and her son.

While a monthly disposable income of 16,000 *kroner* for a mother and son is not lavish – after all, Carina had to pay rent *and* her son's sports-club fee – she was clearly above Karen Hækkerup's official 2013 poverty line. But definitions aside, the 'Poor Carina' debate generally left Danes feeling that cash-benefit recipients are coddled by an indulgent welfare system.

In September 2012, about a year later, 'Lazy Robert' entered the limelight after an impromptu street interview on national television. Robert, also a recipient of social assistance, bluntly explained that he had "a choice at the job centre. Should I take a shitty job at McDonald's that pays 100 *kroner* an hour, or do I want to keep getting cash benefits? And that's where I say: That job is so bad I'd rather be on cash benefits. Otherwise society has to make me an offer that corresponds to the skills and the energy I have."

Viewers may have questioned the skillset of Robert, a self-declared triple university dropout, but he was convinced of his own worth. Again a ruckus ensued, including a reaction from the outspoken Joachim B. Olsen: "This is an insult to all the people who get up [every morning] and take all the jobs Robert doesn't want, and who have to work more and pay higher taxes. This is morally reprehensible."

In my second chapter I concluded that Danes love welfare services because everyone who really needs help is entitled to get it. For many hard-working Danes, Poor Carina and Lazy Robert proved that it was easy to wheedle your way to welfare without being needy, and that the welfare state helps slackers with an inflated sense of entitlement sponge off the communal funds.

Carina and Robert are no longer top news items, although 'Lazy Robert' did earn the national broadcasting corporation's title "DR News Word of the Year" in 2012. Now part of the Danish collective consciousness, these figures, and their aftertaste of insult, typify a lasting shift in the political debate. Advocates of welfare reform have found support to surpass even their wildest dreams, the moral of these stories being: Cash-benefit recipients are lazy and pampered. Time to drop the carrots and get out the stick!

Another good example of this shift may be found in a book by Karina Pedersen entitled *Helt ude i hampen. Mails fra underklassen* (roughly: 'Totally whacked. Emails from the lower class'), which sparked a heated debate in autumn 2016. Karina describes her childhood, living with an unemployed mother in an urban public-housing project with many other residents on cash benefits or early retirement after being assessed as 'unable to work'. The author's message is that the poor do not lack money, they lack moral fibre:

My mother's early retirement has opened up … prospects for her to stick her paws into the public coffers … Somebody ought to take a good look at the country's assessed-early-retirement recipients. Many of them could have avoided a life on benefits, if only they had shown more moderation in their lives.

These winds of moral change coincide with other massive changes. Beginning in the late 2010s, Danish politicians have constantly had to trim the sails and tackle of the welfare state to keep it afloat, never mind moving onwards and upwards. They must deal with refugees, globalisation and an ageing population, as well as coronavirus and other challenges on the horizon. Let us look at how this is affecting the welfare system the Danes love so well.

AND THE FUTURE?

THE TRUSTY OLD BUMBLEBEE

Over the years many have likened the Danish welfare state to a bumblebee. As the saying goes, it cannot fly – but since no one has told it so, it does. So too with the welfare state: How can Denmark's economy continue to stay aloft under the double burden of heavy taxes and a generous, universal welfare system? There must be a secret!

The trusty bumblebee has no idea why it can fly, defying normal aerodynamic theory, but entomologists do. Its secret lies in the rough surface and flexibility of its wings, which give extra lift with each wingbeat.

Similarly, there is no secret behind Denmark's ability to combine welfare, wealth and growth. Social scientists like myself know quite a bit about what makes Denmark tick, although we cannot point to a single decisive factor. The recipe for successfully combining economic growth and universal welfare benefits calls for a variety of ingredients.

The first is a relatively flexible labour market, and Denmark's 'flexicurity' model fits the bill, combining *flexibility* for employers and financial *security* for employees.

This helps Danish companies by enabling them to hire and fire employees more flexibly, and to restructure or downsize more rapidly if times get tough. By contrast, in several continental European countries it is almost impossible to terminate employees. Even after the financial crisis of '08–09 and the economic downturn and social reform that happened in its wake, millions of Italians, Frenchmen and Germans enjoy a level of job security virtually unknown in Denmark today.

But why has Denmark's strong labour movement agreed to give companies such flexible conditions? Because workers got something in return, obviously, in the usual give-and-take of labour relations. Above all, this flexibility has promoted job creation and a healthy national economy. But more importantly, the 'price' of flexibility was generous unemployment benefits and a massive system for further education and training – paid or subsidised by the state. The flexicurity model exemplifies how the welfare state can co-create good framework conditions for the business community.

Another important ingredient in the Danish welfare-state mix is the education system, with publicly funded programmes for all citizens who qualify. This means, in the simplest terms, that the Danish state makes sure companies have access to a qualified workforce.

In Germany and Italy, for instance, companies must organise and fund employee training, and young craftsmen and industrial operators must acquire most basic skills on the job. In Denmark, vocational schools teach young people a basic skillset before turning them loose on the labour market.

The same goes for academic education. Most students in the US, the UK and Australia spend two to three years in college and earn a bachelor's degree, after which their first employer spends time and money on their further education. To some extent this also happens in Denmark, but the basic level among skilled workers and academics is higher for their first entry-level job.

The Danish basic level of primary and lower-secondary education is also higher. Affluent, ambitious American parents often send their children to private schools, lowering the general attainment level in state-run schools. This, in turn, attracts the best teachers to private schools, which offer better wages and more motivated pupils. This system produces a small group of high achievers and a large group of school-leavers with poor academic skills.

Danish private schools are generally less elitist, and the state-run schools cater to a wider variety of pupils. This helps prevent academically weak pupils from falling hopelessly behind, a greater risk in countries where community schools are under pressure. Poorly educated Americans, for instance, are simply worse off academically than poorly educated Danes. As a result, Danish companies have access to a relatively well-qualified labour force, including workers for jobs that do not require specialist training or a higher education.

Childcare is a third ingredient in Denmark's success,

showing how the welfare state can play *with*, rather than *against*, trade and industry. As noted earlier, women make up a large part of the Danish workforce. They can do this because having children does not prevent them from also having a job. Young families in many other countries find work–life balance much more elusive, and women often limit work outside the home, or give it up altogether.

This is not good for companies. It reduces the pool of competent, skilled employees, and much talent is lost. From a strictly fiscal angle, it is not good for the economy either. All else being equal, a smaller workforce means companies must compete harder to get labour when times are good. This can make pay levels rise quickly, in turn making companies less competitive.

Another documented advantage of a well-organised childcare system is that going to kindergarten gives children a variety of social skills that benefit them later in life. They get better at planning and communicating with others, and therefore they generally do better at school. Actually, most of my colleagues agree that one of the best investments any politician can make is to ensure a healthy, wholesome environment for children in crèches and kindergartens. As an independent factor, this has a positive impact on the quality of a country's future workforce.

A WEIGHT, OR A WAVE?

Denmark's robust welfare system is largely a friend of trade and industry, not an enemy. But even stone can crumble, and one of our welfare state's strongest pillars – the assumption that everyone who *can* work *should* work – is under pressure from several sides.

For one thing, the Danish population is aging. Projections from Statistics Denmark show 60-plus-aged citizens rising from 25% in 2016 to 29% in 2030. In the social sciences, researchers call this a 'significant' increase, occurring in less than 15 years. Worse still, the country's core workforce, Danes aged 30–49, will shrink during this period.

A couple of years ago I gave a lecture for some Norwegian students and spoke about this phenomenon, using the common Danish 'burden' phraseology: 'the weight of aging' among the population. Although our languages and societies are quite similar – Norwegians even have *-sen* surnames, and not *-son* surnames, like the Swedes – some in the audience took offence. Norwegians call this 'the wave of aging', and I was tersely informed that elderly citizens are no burden. Shame on me!

Political correctness is not a typical Danish trait, nor is it a personal trait of mine. Besides, I am a researcher, so permit me to be blunt: Old people are expensive.

Above all, they stop working. Various Danish governments have already raised the official retirement age, most recently to 68–70, and modified early-retirement options, but the analysis still holds true: Retired people do not work, hence creating no value for companies and paying no ordinary income tax to the state. Older citizens also need more health-care services, so a scenario with more elderly people means higher welfare costs.

Another factor putting pressure on the Danish welfare system is the large number of jobless immigrants from non-Western countries and their descendants. Among ethnic Danes aged 17–64, the employment rate is around 80%. Among non-Western immigrants in that age group, it is only two thirds of that. Fewer in jobs means less regular income tax for the state, and larger welfare-benefit pay-outs. This means that boosting employment among immigrants and their descendants is one of Denmark's key socio-economic challenges.

Globalisation, digitisation and automation is also reducing the number of non-skilled jobs. Today, industrial products of every kind are often cheaper to manufacture in China or Vietnam, and most 'manual' labour can safely be placed in the hands of sophisticated machines and robots. The number of non-skilled jobs in Denmark has already plummeted, from some 1 million in 1990 to 0.6 million around 2020.

The future of such jobs looks bleak. OECD says about one third of all Danish jobs risk being automated in the future, and the tell-tale signs are all around us: gardeners getting a helping hand from automatic lawnmowers, and bookkeepers using increasingly savvy IT systems. The science-fiction scenarios of yesteryear, complete with robotic housekeepers and self-driving buses, may be real life within the next decade.

It is obviously impossible to predict how technology

will change, and humanity has a tendency to fear the future if it seems uncertain. Even so, if just 10% of the workforce becomes superfluous it will be a highly significant change. This, too, will hit non-skilled workers hardest, all else being equal, since as a group they can be hard to retain and retrain for new, more demanding jobs.

These prospects threaten the bedrock of Denmark's economy, and also endanger the population's willingness to co-finance welfare for all. As I mentioned, a universal welfare system like Denmark's depends on most people working. It is workers who create financial value and pay taxes. When too many people leave the workforce, voluntarily or for other reasons, it threatens the basic cohesion, the brick-and-mortar sturdiness, of the welfare state. Another metaphor, fitting for this seafaring nation, would be: We are all in the same boat, but some of us are manning the oars while others sit on deck under the canopy, enjoying the view.

If 'Poor Carina' and 'Lazy Robert' have taught the Danes anything, it is that we do not like freeloaders. Many feel that if our welfare system promotes or condones shirking, it is time for a change. The people's tribunal – public opinion – is especially tough on immigrants and their descendants. One reason is that many 'old' ethnic Danes do not believe that 'new' Danes have contributed much to the nation's welfare. Another reason, shown in several studies, is that many Danes mix their specific views on the welfare system with their general views on immigration.

Based on this, we can detect a very particular attitude: Welfare benefits for 'new' Danes ought to be less generous than for ethnic Danes. A study by a colleague of mine, Christian Albrekt Larsen, actually shows that a growing majority of Danes would like lower levels of welfare service for immigrants and their descendants than for the rest of the population.

WELFARE STATE 2.0

Predictions are hard to make, especially about the future, as the saying goes. But humour aside, it helps a lot if the future is unfolding right before your eyes. As I see it, rather than a system reboot, Denmark is heading for 'Welfare State 2.0'.

In the boat I just conjured up, ideally everyone takes a turn at the oars. The young and old do not have to row, but only because everyone else rows as hard as they can after childhood and before old age. It's joy and harmony and smooth sailing, with communal singing above and below deck. But lately, more people are never even touching the oars, breaking the social contract that keeps the boat – our society – afloat. This is not sustainable. The solution is simple. To the lifeboats! Let us fend for ourselves, each in our own little dinghy.

This is what Danish politicians have lately been promoting. From all being in the same boat, we are gradually building different boats for different groups in our society. There are two processes at work here: less generous unemployment benefits, and more elements of mutual insurance. As we look at these processes separately, I will take you through some of the sail-roping and tackle-trimming done in recent years to keep Denmark on course. You've made it this far, so grab your gloves: All hands on deck!

In 2010, the first Liberal–Conservative coalition government of Lars Løkke Rasmussen passed a reform (with Social Liberal support) of the benefit coverage for members of an unemployment-insurance scheme. Instead of four years of benefits – at 80% of the recipient's former wage – these people could only receive benefits for two years. After this, a recipient would have to work for 52 weeks (compared to 26 weeks, pre-reform) to once again become entitled to benefit coverage.

This reform was a nuisance for the next government, a centre–left coalition formed by Helle Thorning-Schmidt of the Social Democrats in 2011. But the 'price' for coming to power was accepting the reform. The reform package has since been adjusted several times, and a new political accord reached in 2015 made no fundamental changes.

For jobless people who are not members of an unemployment-insurance scheme, or whose two-year benefit period has expired, there is the state programme of 'social assistance'. This is less than unemployment insurance, and recipients of social assistance must have no personal assets – say, a summer cottage – which they could use or sell to cover their living expenses. As for married recipients, their spouse's income is deducted from the amount they receive, meaning that many jobless people do not qualify for social assistance at all, since their spouse's income is larger than the amount they would be eligible to receive.

So, unemployment insurance *and* social assistance have been reduced in recent years. In 2016 the second government of Lars Løkke Rasmussen – an all-fiscal-conservative Liberal Party minority government – introduced a 'social-assistance ceiling' for the total amount a person can receive from the public coffers.

Before this ceiling was introduced, recipients of social assistance with children got certain extras, such as extra child support, which could give them a fairly high total monthly income. Single parents with one or more children had a ceiling of just over 15,000 *kroner* (2,000 euros) per month to pay taxes, rent, living costs and everything else.

The Economic Council of the Labour Movement estimated that after the social-assistance ceiling, roughly 30,000 people got less public money than before, with 34,000 children living in families whose support is affected.

As per Karen Hækkerup's now-defunct poverty line, the cash-benefit ceiling has made about 16,000 people in Denmark 'poor', including 11,000 children – with minors overrepresented because the ceiling affects the amount of extra child support single parents get.

Lars Løkke Rasmussen's second government also introduced other regulations, including a requirement that recipients of social assistance must work 225 hours per year. If they do not, their benefits are reduced. In addition, a new 'integration benefit' means that jobless people only receive the full amount of social assistance if they have resided in Denmark for at least seven of the last eight years.

With the 'social-assistance ceiling', the '225-hour rule' and the 'integration benefit', politicians have made it "more appealing to find a job", as the Danes put it. For many benefit recipients these measures could be the kind of tough love it takes to get them into gear. But there will always be people who, for various reasons – such as mental illness, or poor language or vocational skills – are unable to find or keep a job. These measures will make their financial situation much worse, perhaps permanently.

My crystal ball shows no signs that Danish politicians will be changing these measure in the near future. The Social Democratic minority government formed in 2019 under Mette Frederiksen has passed certain modifications, but tough love – social-democratic style – is still the order of the day. The 'social-assistance' system, in particular, seems changed for good, and it is no secret that immigrants and their descendants are massively over-represented among its recipients. Most Danes have no problem making life a little harder for this group.

By trimming the benefits 'new Danes' get, the politicians can free up money to give their core voters more nice welfare services: tax breaks, new mega-hospitals or more helping hands to care for the elderly. The social-assistance ceiling and the 225-hour rule, for example, free up about 500 million *kroner* a year in public funds – quite a large sum for such a small economy. And I could easily imagine future politicians being tempted to find easy money by trimming the benefits of unpopular recipient groups.

Now let us look at the second process: more private welfare insurance. In a Danish context, this means people drawing up pension or insurance plans for themselves, beyond what the welfare society offers everyone.

The most important new insurance element in recent decades is the 'labour-market pensions', now a cornerstone in the Danish welfare system. Invented in 1989, these pensions have grown to include many wage earners. In my case, for instance, I pay 17.1% of my monthly salary into my labour-market pension. Well, actually, I don't. An automatic system does, and I cannot tell it *not* to.

The labour-market pensions greatly enhanced the level of Danish welfare. The universal old-age pension of some 12,000 *kroner* (1,600 euros) is fairly modest, so people with no extra pension are often hard hit financially when they retire. But the side effect of saving 17.1% of one's work income over a lifetime is that those who earn more, like doctors or engineers, automatically save more, especially compared to low earners like health-care assistants or social educators. Hence, the financial inequality on the labour market is reflected in people's pension incomes and well-being in old age.

The number of private health insurance policies has also swelled. Back in 2002, fiscal conservative Anders Fogh Rasmussen of the Liberal Party, then prime minister, introduced a tax deduction that made private health insurance policies less expensive. From just a few thousand, the number skyrocketed to 1.5 million in 2012 – the year social-democratic Helle Thorning-Schmidt scrapped the deduction. Most economists expected this to reverse the trend, but as of 2019 the number was 2 million.

This surge is remarkable, keeping in mind that all 5.8 million Danes are entitled to universal care in the nation's high-quality health system. But private insurance holders can access diagnosis and treatment faster than the rest of the population. Though not morally reprehensible, this does divide Danes into what we often call an 'A team' and a 'B team' in terms of health-care access and privileges.

My crystal ball shows no signs of this trend stopping any time soon either, although I predict it will soon reach a plateau. But those who are insured will merely shift to demanding coverage of more, and costlier, tests and treatment, further skewing the difference between private and public services.

Besides these two processes, a third factor, apolitical but akin to labour-market pensions and private health insurance, is the growing number of pupils in privately run schools, most from solid 'A team' backgrounds. In just five years, 2011–2016, the number of pupils aged 6–16 in private schools rose by over 10,000, even while the total number of Danish pupils shrank by about 5,000.

All in all, this portends a Danish future in which communal services increasingly become catch-all programmes for those who cannot pay for private extras or alternatives. This will only create more inequality in the welfare services each individual Dane can access.

On the other hand, the rumours of the welfare state's death are greatly exaggerated. Danes continue to give strong support to the national health system, care for the elderly, free education and subsidised public childcare. The only thing is, we do not want to share these things with people unlike us. Nor do we wish to pay for other welfare services and benefits than the ones our families use now, or may use in the future.

It is beyond doubt that the Danish model is changing in terms of the welfare it guarantees and delivers to it citizens. More than before, services and benefits are being targeted to the middle class. And in the future, people who have less education or are marginalised, and immigrants and their descendants, will get fewer welfare services than before, which will benefit the middle class. In other words, Denmark will no doubt continue to deliver first-class welfare – just not to everyone in equal measure.